Making Tally Charts

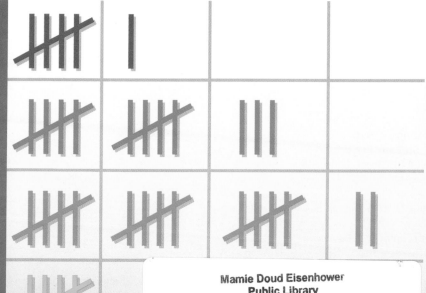

By Elizabeth Whyte

Gareth Stevens
PUBLISHING

[leveled
reader]
math

Please visit our website, www.garethstevens.com. For a free color catalog of all our high-quality books, call toll free 1-800-542-2595 or fax 1-877-542-2596.

Library of Congress Cataloging-in-Publication Data

Whyte, Elizabeth.
Making Tally Charts / by Elizabeth Whyte.
 p. cm. — (Graph it!)
Includes index.
ISBN 978-1-4824-0845-4 (pbk.)
ISBN 978-1-4824-0879-9 (6-pack)
ISBN 978-1-4824-0844-7 (library binding)
1. Mathematics — Graphic methods — Juvenile literature. 2. Mathematics — Charts, diagrams, etc. — Juvenile literature. 3. Tallies — Juvenile literature. I. Whyte, Elizabeth. II. Title.
QA40.5 W536 2015
510—d23

Published in 2015 by
Gareth Stevens Publishing
111 East 14th Street, Suite 349
New York, NY 10003

Copyright © 2015 Gareth Stevens Publishing

Designer: Katelyn E. Reynolds
Editor: Therese Shea

Photo credits: Cover, pp. 1–24 (background texture) ctrlaplus/Shutterstock.com; cover, p. 5 Jupiterimages/Pixland/Thinkstock.com; pp. 1, 7, 9, 11, 13, 17, 19, 21 (tally chart elements) Colorlife/Shutterstock.com; p. 15 (all) leonello calvetti/Shutterstock.com; p. 17 (photo) Tomwang112/iStock/Thinkstock.com.

Printed in the United States of America

CPSIA compliance information: Batch #CS15GS: For further information contact Gareth Stevens, New York, New York at 1-800-542-2595.

Contents

Boldface words appear in the glossary.

Tally It Up!

A tally is a mark that stands for 1. Tallies are used to count. Tally charts are a fun way to **compare** amounts. Let's learn how to read tally charts. Then, you can make one of your own!

4

tally

5

Question and Answer

Tally charts help us **record** answers to questions. Imagine someone asked friends where they had their birthday party. This tally chart shows the answers. Each tally stands for one person's answer. Which place had the most parties? Check your answer on page 22.

Where Was Your Birthday Party?

place	number of people
Pizza Palace	|||
Park Place Playground	||
City Zoo	||||

The Fifth Tally

In a tally chart, every fifth tally is written in a special way. It's drawn across the other four marks to make a group of five. Look at the tallies on the next page. Which number fits in the bottom right box, 8 or 11?

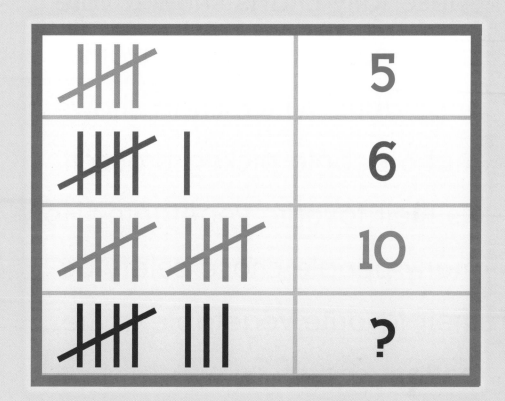

‖‖‖	5
‖‖‖ I	6
‖‖‖ ‖‖‖	10
‖‖‖ III	?

9

These tally charts show a vote about some people's favorite vegetable. Which chart shows that 6 people picked broccoli as their favorite vegetable? How many people chose celery as their favorite vegetable in the bottom chart?

10

Favorite Vegetable

vegetable	number of votes
broccoli	卌 l
carrots	卌 卌
celery	lll

Favorite Vegetable

vegetable	number of votes
broccoli	卌
carrots	卌 l
celery	llll

11

Tons of Tallies

Tally charts help us record a large number of votes. Sets of five are easier to count than ones. This tally chart shows students' votes for best teacher. Which teacher received the most votes? How many votes did that teacher receive?

Best Teacher

teacher	number of votes
Mr. Albertson	## ## ##
Ms. O'Mara	## ## ## ||||
Mrs. Woods	## ## |
Mr. Suarez	## ## ## |||

Time to Tally Dinosaurs

Imagine you want to find out which are the most **popular** dinosaurs among your friends. You can make a tally chart. Ask your friends to choose a favorite from these four dinosaurs: *Tyrannosaurus rex, Triceratops, Allosaurus,* and *Stegosaurus.*

Tyrannosaurus rex

Stegosaurus

Allosaurus

Triceratops

Draw your tally chart on a piece of paper. Write a title such as "Most Popular Dinosaurs" on top. Make two columns under it. Label one column "kind of dinosaur." Write the name of each dinosaur below. Label the other column "number of votes."

Most Popular Dinosaurs

kind of dinosaur	number of votes
Tyrannosaurus rex	
Triceratops	
Allosaurus	
Stegosaurus	

Imagine 12 friends voted for *Tyrannosaurus rex*, 15 for *Triceratops*, 11 for *Allosaurus*, and 6 for *Stegosaurus*. Put the tally marks in your chart. It should look like this chart. How many more friends voted for *Tyrannosaurus rex* than *Stegosaurus*?

Most Popular Dinosaurs

kind of dinosaur	number of votes
Tyrannosaurus rex	~~||||~~ ~~||||~~ ||
Triceratops	~~||||~~ ~~||||~~ ~~||||~~
Allosaurus	~~||||~~ ~~||||~~	
Stegosaurus	~~||||~~	

Tally Charts and Bar Graphs

A tally chart can be used to make a bar graph. This tally chart and bar graph show the same facts about how a class raised money for a trip. What activity did most students do to raise money? Now, make your own tally chart!

Class Trip Activity

kind of activity	number of students
car wash	⫴⫴⫴ ‖
bake sale	⫴⫴⫴
dance	‖
yard sale	⫴⫴⫴ ǀ

Class Trip Activity

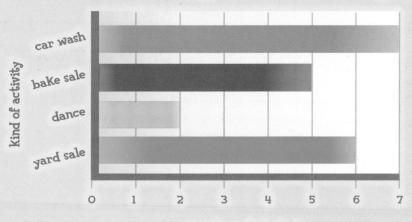

Glossary

compare: to find what is the same and what is different about two or more things

popular: liked by many people

record: to make a note of something so it can be remembered

Answer Key

p. 6 City Zoo

p. 8 8

p. 10 chart on top, 4 people

p. 12 Ms. O'Mara, 19 votes

p. 18 6 more friends

p. 20 car wash

For More Information

Books

Cocca, Lisa Colozza. *Tally Charts*. Ann Arbor, MI: Cherry Lake Publishing, 2013.

Edgar, Sherra G. *Tally Charts*. Ann Arbor, MI: Cherry Lake Publishing, 2013.

Nelson, Robin. *Let's Make a Tally Chart*. Minneapolis, MN: Lerner Publications, 2013.

Websites

Interpret Data in Tally Charts, Picture Graphs, Tables
www.ixl.com/math/grade-1/interpret-data-in-tally-charts-picture-graphs-tables
Answer questions about tally charts and more.

Tally Charts and Bar Graphs
www.brainpopjr.com/math/data/tallychartsandbargraphs/
Watch a video about surveys and tally charts.

Index

24